I Wear Teal For My Mom

by

Kristy Rhodes

Illustrations by Sue Lynn Cotton

the PeppertreePress LLC

Sarasota, Florida

For information regarding permission,
call 941-922-2662 or contact us at our website:
www.peppertreepublishing.com or write to:
the Peppertree Press, LLC.
Attention: Publisher
1269 First Street, Suite 7
Sarasota, Florida 34236

ISBN: 978-1-61493-789-0

Library of Congress Number: 2021919955

Printed October 2021

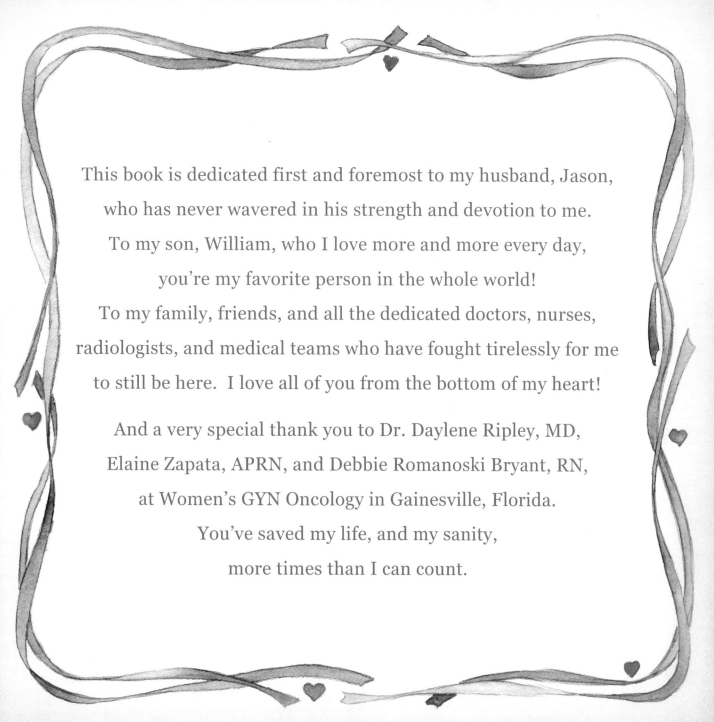

This book is dedicated first and foremost to my husband, Jason,
who has never wavered in his strength and devotion to me.
To my son, William, who I love more and more every day,
you're my favorite person in the whole world!
To my family, friends, and all the dedicated doctors, nurses,
radiologists, and medical teams who have fought tirelessly for me
to still be here. I love all of you from the bottom of my heart!

And a very special thank you to Dr. Daylene Ripley, MD,
Elaine Zapata, APRN, and Debbie Romanoski Bryant, RN,
at Women's GYN Oncology in Gainesville, Florida.
You've saved my life, and my sanity,
more times than I can count.

My name is William and I live in a house with
my Mommy, Daddy, and our cat named Friday.

One day Mommy didn't feel good and
Daddy took her to the doctor.

When they came home they were very sad.
Mommy had Ovarian Cancer and had to have a big operation.

Daddy told me that Mommy was going to be just fine but that things would be a little bit different for a while.

The day before her operation
Mommy and I made cupcakes!
We cuddled a lot and I got lots of
extra hugs and kisses.

For the next few days Grandma and Grandpa
took care of me and we played outside a lot!

After a few days in the hospital Mommy came home!
She had a big bandage over the boo-boo on her tummy.
I had to be very careful with Mommy and give her "baby"
hugs and kisses. No running into her or jumping on her.

Mommy took lots of naps. Daddy said that taking lots of naps would help Mommy's tummy get better faster.

Daddy made dinner every night while Mommy napped.
Sometimes friends and family dropped off meals
that were already cooked for us!
It made me happy to have
people thinking about us.

It wasn't long before Mommy was feeling well enough to play like we used to. But I still had to be careful to not jump on her.

Soon Mommy had to start chemotherapy (kee-moh-ther-uh-pee). This is a special medicine to help her get better. She had something called a "port" where the medicine went in.

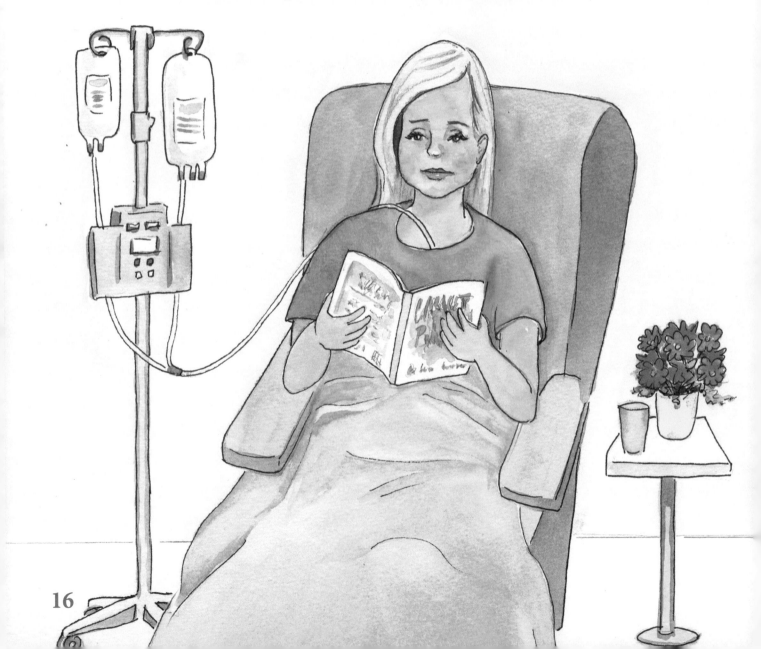

The doctor who gives Mommy
the chemotherapy is called an
Oncologist (ong-kol-uh-jist).

The chemotherapy made Mommy very tired and
sometimes she had a tummy ache like
she ate too much candy.

The chemotherapy also made Mommy's hair fall out. This is called alopecia (al-uh-pee-shee-uh). This made her very sad but Daddy took her to a special store to buy a wig and she was still my pretty Mommy!

Mommy had to have chemotherapy for what seemed like forever but soon she was all done and the cancer went into remission (ri-mish-uhn). This meant that the chemotherapy worked and the cancer was all gone!

Mommy's hair soon started to grow back and she felt better and better every day. She only had to visit her doctor once in a while.

I'm so thankful to have my Mommy and I wear **teal** for her!

22

Discussion Questions

1)   What was your favorite part of the book?

2)   What was your least favorite part of the book?

3)   How did you feel when William's mom got sick?

4)   How did you feel seeing William's friends and family help take care of him and his dad when his mom got sick?

5)   Do you know any real people like William's family?

6)   What did you learn from William's story?

CPSIA information can be obtained
at www.ICGtesting.com
Printed in the USA
BVHW021746081121
621108BV00001B/4